Original title:
Saplings of the Soul

Copyright © 2025 Creative Arts Management OÜ
All rights reserved.

Author: Miriam Kensington
ISBN HARDBACK: 978-1-80567-453-5
ISBN PAPERBACK: 978-1-80567-752-9

Embracing the Dawn

In the morning light, we stretch and yawn,
A dance begins with sleepy fawn.
Coffee brews, it makes us cheer,
Even squirrels in trees seem to leer.

Jammies on, we face the day,
With cereal crumbs leading us astray.
In this gleeful, wacky race,
We wear our smiles, a silly grace.

Whispered Promises of Spring

Buds are popping, it's quite the sight,
Bumblebees buzzing, a fanciful flight.
Tulips giggle, waving so spry,
While daffodils sport bows, oh my!

Rain boots stomp in puddles wide,
Rainbows stretch, they're full of pride.
Nature's giggles fill the air,
As birds wear hats without a care.

In the Shade of Starlit Dreams

Under stars that flash and wink,
The moon takes notes, it loves to think.
Crickets chirp their late-night tune,
While owls hoot, saying, 'We're in bloom!'

Fireflies dance in a curious trance,
While shadows plot a jumping chance.
A picnic blankie starts to sway,
As midnight snickers at the play.

Awakening the Inner Garden

Inside our hearts, the seeds do sprout,
With giggles and wiggles, there's no doubt.
We plant our dreams in silly rows,
Watered with laughter, that's how it goes.

Sunshine smiles, it tickles our skin,
While butterflies giggle, let's spin!
With weeds that tease and flowers that sway,
Our gardens bloom in the quirkiest way.

Sunlit Paths of Renewal

On a path where shadows play,
A squirrel skitters, bright and gay.
Who knew that acorns were such snacks?
With nutty laughter, the forest cracks!

Sunshine tickles trees so tall,
Where giggles bounce and shimmers fall.
A dance of leaves, a twirl of fun,
As all the critters bask in sun!

Echoing Forests of the Heart

In the woods where echoes sing,
A rabbit hops on jiggly spring.
With thumping feet, it leads the way,
To find a party at the bay!

Trees are clapping, oh what joy!
Joining in, each girl and boy.
With silly hats, they jump and swirl,
In forests where the laughter twirls!

Seeds of Tomorrow's Echo

Tiny seeds with dreams to grow,
Sprout a giggle, put on a show.
With sprigs of humor, tall as clouds,
They wear their leaves like playful shrouds!

Roots that tickle underground,
Where worms and bugs all laugh around.
Tiny voices whisper clear,
"We're here to spread some joy and cheer!"

Lullabies of Whispering Leaves

Gentle breezes play their tune,
As leaves sway under the bright moon.
Each rustle sparks a lullaby,
That makes the sleeping critters sigh!

But wait! A raccoon steals the show,
With acrobats like none we know.
As twinkling stars laugh high above,
The forest hums with dreams of love!

Petals on the Wind

Blowing bubbles of laughter,\nPetals dance all around,\nEach giggle a soft whisper,\nIn this playful sound.

Frisky breezes tease flowers,\nTickling them just right,\nWith every twist and turn,\nThey sway in pure delight.

Who knew blooms could chuckle?\nThey scatter jokes like seeds,\nSprouting smiles in gardens,\nMeeting all our needs.

So lift your heart in laughter,\nLet petals paint the skies,\nFor a world full of giggles,\nIs the best of all ties.

A Symphony of Fresh Starts

In the morning's bright embrace,\nNew leaves unfurl their dreams,\nA jolly orchestra plays loud,\nLife's laughter in their beams.

Roots dig deep in friendly soil,\nTickling worms below,\nEach sprout's a quirky solo,\nIn nature's lively show.

Branches sway like dancers,\nWaving hands in fun,\nA symphony of fresh starts,\nWith every rising sun.

So take a bow, dear sproutlings,\nEmbrace your vast potential,\nFor every twist and turn explored,\nBears fruits quite essential.

When Seasons Change Inside

Oh, winter's chill is silly,\nWith snowflakes in a swirl,\nWhile springtime plans its pranks,\nAnd little buds unfurl.

Summer shouts with laughter,\nWhile autumn starts to tease,\nIt juggles leaves like confetti,\nSending smiles like the breeze.

Each season more capricious,\nAs days begin to blend,\nA waltz of time and nature,\nWhere every leaf's a friend.

So when you feel the changes,\nJust giggle and enjoy,\nFor life's a lively song,\nA chorus of pure joy.

Garden of Silent Aspirations

In corners where dreams gather,\nInvisible roots entwine,\nThis garden keeps on chuckling,\nWhile tiny sparks align.

Whispers float on dainty air,\nWith secrets held in twigs,\nPlants ponder their wild hopes,\nIn a world of little digs.

A sunflower winks at daisies,\nWith plans of grandeur tall,\nWhile clovers share their giggles,\nOne and all, one and all.

So tend to quiet visions,\nWith laughter as your tool,\nFor in this merry garden,\nHope sprouts—oh, how it's cool!

Chasing Sunbeams and Shadows

In the garden of giggles, they leap and play,
Chasing sunbeams, running away.
With shadows that dance and twist in the light,
They giggle and tumble, what a sight!

The daisies are laughing, the daisies agree,
That chasing their shadows is key to be free.
With each little tumble, they find new delight,
In the game of the sun, oh, what a delight!

Nature's Tender Caress

Leaves whisper softly, a tickle on skin,
While squirrels do cartwheels, oh, where to begin?
The flowers confetti their colors so bright,
While bees do the hustle, oh what a sight!

A breeze full of chuckles, nature's own joke,
Finds laughter in pines as they sway and poke.
There's no greater comfort than nature's embrace,
With funny little critters that quicken the pace!

Fostering the Unseen

In the mud, the worms wiggle, a secret parade,
While ants march in line, a tiny charade.
Invisible magic in every small nook,
Who knew little beetles could write their own book?

The fungi are chuckling, a playful delight,
As fairies do pirouettes under the moonlight.
With each hidden laughter, the world comes alive,
In the garden of chaos, the giggles will thrive!

In the Cradle of Growth

Little sprouts giggle, peek out from the ground,
With dreams of becoming so tall and so round.
They stretch for the sunshine, wiggle with glee,
In the cradle of dirt, they grow wild and free!

With raindrop confetti, their party begins,
The roots do the tango, oh, where do we spin?
In the soil's warm embrace, laughter's unfurled,
Nature's own party, oh, welcome to the world!

Heartstrings of the Earth

A worm told a joke to a clumsy bee,
The punchline flew high, like a runaway spree.
Rabbits hopped in, with ears flopped down,
While the daisies giggled, wearing their crown.

The soil chuckled, tickled by rain,
Telling old tales of sunshine and pain.
Grass blades danced, they formed a long line,
Swaying together, like they're sipping wine.

Nurtured Dreams Take Flight

A seed whispered secrets to a sprout nearby,
"Let's grow some wings and learn how to fly!"
The roots shook with laughter, they wiggled with glee,
"Dreams of the sky? Oh, just wait and see!"

Bouncing on clouds, they made silly faces,
Chasing down rainbows, they won all the races.
With nutty ideas, they spun round and round,
All giggles and joy in the garden they found.

Beneath the Surface

Down in the dirt, there's a thumping surprise,
The moles are hosting their underground pies.
With worms as the band, playing tunes so slick,
Even the roots couldn't help but do tricks.

"Join in the fun!" cries a beetle with flair,
As daisies peer down, trying hard not to stare.
A show of the underground, known only to few,
With laughter that tickles the roots where they grew.

Life Awakens

In springtime's giggle, the flowers awake,
With sunglasses on, they dance by the lake.
A picnic of petals, spreads out on the grass,
While the sun plays tag with a cheeseball of brass.

Every beep of a bee sends them into a spin,
With a flutter and buzz, the fun can begin.
Sipping sweet nectar from cups made of blooms,
The garden's a party, all laughter and zooms.

Growing Pains of the Spirit

A young tree complained, "I feel rather tall,
But my branches are silly, they've no sense at all!"
The breeze gave a chuckle, and rustled its leaves,
"Just go with the flow; it's how life achieves!"

In the dark of the night, stars twinkled bright,
Encouraging whispers, "You're a wonderful sight."
The tree gave a grin, shook off all its fright,
And danced with the moon, till the day turned to light.

The Caress of Nature's Breath

In the meadow where daisies sway,
A bee buzzes, it's here to play.
It sneezes pollen, oh what a sight,
Allergies lurking, ready to bite!

The trees giggle with leaves that dance,
While squirrels plot their daring prance.
A breeze chuckles, tickles my ear,
"Don't worry friend, nature's good cheer!"

A snail in a shell, moves at a crawl,
While grasshoppers hold a grand ball.
They leap and frolic, with no care,
While I sit back, without a spare!

Yet in this chaos, I find a peace,
Nature's laughter will never cease.
So I join in the joyous jest,
As the heart of the wild puts me to rest.

Streams of Tranquility

The river chuckles under the sun,
It splashes joy, oh what fun!
With every ripple, a silly face,
"I'm the king of this watery place!"

The fish wiggle in a dance so fine,
They swim in circles like a line.
One jumps high, a flopping jest,
"Catch me if you can, I'm the best!"

With ducks that quack in rhythmic beats,
And turtles bobbing to nature's feats.
Each twist and turn, a game anew,
As laughter bubbles, who needs a clue?

The stream whispers secrets, soft and sweet,
To every critter, it's quite a treat.
So join the laughter, let spirits soar,
In these waters, we are forevermore.

Vines of Connection

Climbing high, the ivy twirls,
With every twist, it gives a whirl.
"Who needs a ladder?" it scoffs with glee,
"Nature's my home, just look at me!"

A rabbit hops by with a grin so wide,
"I've got the best munchies on this side!"
While garden gnomes gossip in a row,
"Did you see that vine? It's quite the show!"

The sun peeks through, a wink in its rays,
Giving a nod to mischievous plays.
Vines wrap and roll, a tangled fun,
As laughter echoes, second to none!

In this green world where stories twine,
We share a giggle, oh how divine!
So climb the vines and join the spree,
In this patch of joy, you're wild and free.

The Lyrical Bud

A bud pops open, with a yawning stretch,
"Hey, world! It's me, your newest wretch!"
Beneath the sun, it starts to hum,
"Let's make this garden feel like a drum!"

Petals twirl like they're in a dance,
While bees buzz on, giving their chance.
"Care for a sip of this nectar sweet?
It's a flowery party, come take a seat!"

Butterflies whisper, "Let's plot a tour,
To the garden's edge, it's never a bore!"
They flit about, in colors bright,
While the bud chuckles, feeling just right.

So let's embrace this floral cheer,
In the symphony of blooms, we hold dear.
With laughter in petals, under the sky,
We blossom together, oh my, oh my!

Whispers of New Beginnings

In the garden of my mind, I sow,
Tiny thoughts in rows, watch them grow.
They sprout and giggle, dance in the breeze,
Tickling my brain like ants on cheese.

A seed of laughter, a splash of cheer,
Sprouts in my heart, it's crystal clear.
Each silly moment, a bud on a vine,
Grows into a chuckle, oh so divine.

The Roots that Bind

With roots that tickle and intertwine,
They prank each other, oh how they shine.
One says, "I'll trip you, just wait and see!"
But the other replies, "Not on my tree!"

They dig in the dirt, a friendly fight,
Who can grow taller? Oh, what a sight!
Each root a story, a tale of their woe,
Laughing through struggles, they steal the show.

Tender Shoots of Hope

Sprouting up in the laughter-filled air,
Little dreams wobble without a care.
Bouncing and tumbling, they giggle aloud,
Exclaiming, "We're hopeful!" with roots that are proud.

If life hands you raindrops, make slick slides,
Laughing through puddles, take joyful rides.
For tender shoots whisper of possible springs,
Where happiness sprouts, oh, the joy it brings!

Echoes in the Canopy

In the leafy heights, echoes of cheer,
Branches hold secrets, and giggles we hear.
Leaves sway in rhythm, a dance of delight,
Nature's own concert under the moonlight.

The canopy chuckles, a grand old tree,
It says to the saplings, "Come play with me!"
Echoes of joy in the rustling sounds,
Laughter like music, in nature it bounds.

A Symphony in Green

In a garden where plants dance,
They sway to the breeze's prance.
A cactus tried to join the fun,
But ended up poking everyone.

The daisies laughed, the tulips grinned,
As the lively leaves began to spin.
A gnome on break from his old task,
Sipped lemonade and wore a mask.

The trees began a rhythmic sway,
Singing songs of yesterday.
But a squirrel stole the show, you see,
With acorn juggling by the tree.

So when you walk through verdant aisles,
Remember to chuckle; nature smiles.
Each plant's a note in life's grand song,
Where even the weeds still dance along.

Beneath the Boughs of Wonder

Beneath the trees, the chatter grows,
The ants debate on where to pose.
A snail, wearing a leaf like a cape,
Claims he's the hero of the landscape.

Pinecones plot a prank, it's true,
On the unsuspecting birds that flew.
But the owls just hoot, unimpressed,
As they watch the chaos unconfessed.

Mushrooms giggle, hiding their glee,
While pillbugs waltz by the old oak tree.
Each root has tales that wiggle and curl,
In the secret world beneath this swirl.

So lean in close, and you may hear,
Whispers of laughter floating near.
The world beneath the leafy crown,
Is a funny place, with joy abound.

Heartstrings of the Earth

In the meadow, where laughter blooms,
A dandelion dreams in sunlit rooms.
Bees buzz by, in a disco dive,
To keep the heartbeat of spring alive.

A worm plays bass, with rhythm profound,
While crickets chirp the catchy sound.
The flowers sway, donning a grin,
As petals twirl in a dizzy spin.

Rocky the frog croaks a tune,
Underneath a bright, fluffy moon.
While ladybugs dance: two-step, no less,
In the heart of the grass, their fancy dress.

So hum along with the earth's great choir,
Embrace the joy and never tire.
For in this garden, hilarity grows,
With heartstrings woven in each flower that shows.

Journeying through Sprouts

In a pot, two sprouts had a fight,
Over who'd reach for the most sunlight.
One claimed, 'You're just a weed in disguise!'
While the other shot back, 'I'm full of surprise!'

They journeyed up to the garden gate,
With a fork for a guide, they couldn't wait.
A radish in armor gave them a ride,
Through a world of veggies, side by side.

Tomatoes were gossiping, 'A juicy tale!'
As cucumbers rolled in, leaving a trail.
But the sprouts just snickered, enjoying the view,
Beneath the broad leaves that shimmered with dew.

So as they grow, watch their antics unfold,
In the vegetable patch, where stories are told.
Join in the fun on this sprouting spree,
And let every seed dance wild and free.

The Horizon of Inner Light

Little hopes sprout in the dark,
Wiggling about like a curious lark.
They trip on dreams that are silly and bright,
Chasing the moon with all of their might.

With giggles and snorts, they grow tall,
In the garden of thoughts where they bumble and sprawl.
Laughter the water, sunshine the fun,
Planting good vibes until the day's done.

They whisper to clouds, 'Can you see our dance?'
Funky little sprouts, taking their chance.
With roots in the earth and heads in the air,
Jumping and jiving without a single care.

So here's to the dreams that sprout from our core,
Like popcorn in kettles, always wanting more.
Each chuckle a seed, each giggle a gift,
In the landscape of joy, our spirits can lift.

A Dance Among the Shadows

Twilight whispers, 'Let's have a ball,'
Where shadows stretch and the giggles enthrall.
Tiny figures prance, in moonlit delight,
Each twist and turn a comical sight.

They trip on their roots, then tumble with glee,
Doing the chicken with their friends, you see?
A conga of leaves, a shimmy so sweet,
In the land of the wobbly, they dance on their feet.

The wind sings a tune, humorous and bright,
Encouraging sprouts to dance through the night.
Unlikely friendships of branches and twigs,
All join the party with their funky jigs.

Wild little giggles harmonize in the air,
Fluffy clouds join in without a care.
They shimmy and sway, a raucous parade,
In a festival of cheer, their laughter displayed.

Branches Reaching for the Sky

Branches are stretching, like arms in the sun,
They bend and they sway, oh, what a run!
Tiptoeing upwards, with a brave little grin,
Trying to tickle the clouds, let the fun begin.

'Look at me, mom!' they eagerly shout,
'I'm taller than you!' as they twist and sprout.
Their leafy confetti falls down with a plop,
A party for critters that just cannot stop.

Each laugh is a leaf that dances in spring,
With playful little breezes, they giggle and sing.
Branches high fiving, what a silly sight,
As they stretch and they reach with all of their might.

So here's to the moments, while hands wave so free,
In the wild panorama of our leafy spree.
Together they flourish, under the wide sky,
With joy in their hearts, and twinkles that fly.

Resilient Hearts and Fragile Roots

In a plot of good humor, where smiles bloom bright,
Tiny hearts march on, with all of their might.
Fragile but funny, they try to prevail,
Wobbling fiercely, like the wind in a sail.

When life gives them storms, they giggle and wiggle,
Bouncing like puppies that love to sniggle.
With roots deep in laughter and leaves in the air,
They face every challenge with a whimsical flair.

Embracing the tumble, with halos of cheer,
Each little sprout shows no hint of fear.
They play games with shadows, poke fun at the sun,
Twirling and swirling, oh, what stupid fun!

So raise up your glasses to those who stand tall,
With resilient hearts that can weather it all.
In the garden of joy, they blossom and cheer,
For laughter and love shall conquer all fear.

Season of Endless Possibility

In spring, we plant our dreams with flair,
Each seed a wish in the open air.
We water hope, add sunshine's smile,
While dodging mud pies thrown with style.

A squirrel steals the last of our seeds,
Claiming gourmet brunch instead of feeds.
We wave him off, with laughter loud,
As dandelions pop up, allied and proud.

Who knew weeds were quite so spry?
As I tried to plant, they waved goodbye.
Each little sprout brings joy and jest,
Even the bugs think they're the best!

Underneath the Canopy

Beneath the leaves, where shadows play,
The world's a circus, come what may.
Squirrels juggle nuts with flair,
While turtles crawl at a leisurely wear.

The branches creak, the branches sway,
Is that a campfire? No, it's a stray!
A raccoon's feast keeps raccoons awake,
As twinkling stars join in for a break.

"Oops! I dropped my berry pie!"
A shout, a laugh, a bird flew by.
Nature's hilarity brings us cheer,
As we toast to joy with root beer.

Flowers of Forgotten Melodies

In garden plots where tunes forgot,
The blooms begin a giggling trot.
A daisy hums a jaunty tune,
While tulips dance beneath the moon.

A bumblebee joins the sing-along,
As daisies sway to the silly song.
Their petals twirl, oh what a sight,
It's a floral rave on a Friday night!

Violets whisper, "We've got the beat,"
While marigolds shuffle their little feet.
Every flower has a jolly tale,
In a tune-filled land where laughter prevails.

Healing in the Heartwood

In ancient trees, where whispers dwell,
The wood sings soft, a secret spell.
A chipmunk chirps, "Hey, how's it grow?"
While branches sway, putting on a show.

A wooden bench, our throne of dreams,
It creaks and moans, or so it seems.
We sit and chat, share stories old,
And let laughter bloom, bright and bold.

The wise old trunk holds secrets tight,
While squirrels plot their heists at night.
With giggles ringing in the wood,
Our hearts heal well, and life feels good.

Ties That Ground Us

Little roots tickle the toes,
As we dance in garden rows.
Twirling leaves in silly cheer,
Whispering secrets only we hear.

Silly squirrels plot their schemes,
While stretching out their fuzzy dreams.
The sun shines bright, who needs a hat?
When the branches wave like a playful cat!

Worms giggle in their earthy beds,
Sharing tales of their leafy threads.
Punching holes in the dirt so fine,
Creating riddles in the grapevine.

Later we'll sip on dew drops sweet,
And share our stories 'round the beet.
With laughter sprouting all around,
We'll find our humor in the ground.

Life's Hidden Flourish

Underneath the leafy spread,
A garden dance is gently said.
With ants in tuxedos, ready to waltz,
They prance on pathways, not at fault.

In between the blooms so bright,
A snail wears pearls—what a silly sight!
With each slow slide, they make a joke,
And tickle flowers till they choke.

The daisies giggle, petals swaying,
While bees hum tunes, sweetly playing.
A dance-off breaks out, everyone spins,
As earthworms clap with silly grins.

Hidden laughter fills the space,
Each corner hosts a playful race.
Life's secrets sprout, joyful and bold,
In every nook, a tale unfolds.

Echoing Promises in the Earth

Beneath the dirt, a whisper grows,
Of buttercups in fancy clothes.
A promise made with every sprout,
To turn this patch into a shout!

The pickle jars offer sage advice,
"Keep it crunchy, that's your spice!"
Petunias gossip about last week,
Spreading tales that make us squeak!

A parade of bugs takes center stage,
In mossy boots, they act their age.
They twirl and spin with great delight,
Creating echoes on moonlit night.

Promises linger in the air,
As laughter dances without a care.
They tickle roots and spark the mirth,
In the soil, where joy finds its berth.

The Dance of New Beginnings

Tiny buds pop with a grin,
Emerging life, let the fun begin!
A wiggly worm takes the lead,
As daisies follow, fulfilling the need.

With drops of rain, we splash and play,
Giggling under a cloudy gray.
The sun peeks out, a cheeky smile,
Clouds parting, staying for a while.

Jumping seeds burst out of delight,
Making a ruckus all through the night.
As moonbeams tickle the sleepy trees,
The world awakens with gentle ease.

New beginnings are quite the dance,
With every sprout, a silly prance.
We'll twirl and laugh, let our hearts sing,
As all of nature joins the fling!

Inner Landscapes of the Brave

In a garden of giggles, I stand tall,
With weeds as my friends, we're having a ball.
We plot little schemes, like squirrels in the leaves,
And wave at the clouds, dressed in silly sheaves.

With roots that are tangled in mischief and cheer,
I dance with the daisies, and hold back a sneer.
The soil laughs back, with a wink and a nudge,
As we joke with the breeze, never one to judge.

Burgeoning Spirit Amidst Adversity.

When storms pass through, with their thunderous fuss,
I make little boats, from the leaves I can trust.
In puddles we float, like sailors so bold,
With laughter as treasure, a fortune untold.

Each raindrop's a tickle, a dash of good luck,
While mud holds our feet, like gum on a truck.
We splash on and off, like a playful attack,
While the universe smiles, sending giggles back.

Whispers in the Green

In the forest of chuckles, the trees gently sway,
They whisper their secrets in a comical way.
The mushrooms are chatting, with hats on their heads,
While the tall poplars gossip about garden beds.

Here, chortles are carried on a warm summer breeze,
And the flowers are pinching the bees on the knees.
Each petal erupts with a joke of the day,
As nature's own jesters come out to play.

Budding Dreams in Dappled Light

In sunny spots where the giggles ignite,
Tiny dreams sprout, like stars in the night.
Each new little thought is a dance on the ground,
In a world made of whimsy, where laughter is found.

With dappled light sparkling, like fairies that sing,
We twirl with our hopes, that like daisies take wing.
Each bud is a dream that bursts forth with glee,
In this garden of fun, we're just wild and free.

Opened to the Wind

When the breeze tickles leaves so green,
They dance and twist, quite the scene.
Oh, little sprouts, with giggles they sway,
As the wind whispers secrets of play.

Bugs on a mission, they zoom and fly,
But these tiny greens just want to try.
They're plotting a party, or so it seems,
Admiring their roots, fulfilling their dreams.

In puddles they splash, with mud on their cheeks,
Singing their laughter through whistling weeks.
Giggling with daisies, they form a parade,
A comedy act in the theater glade.

So let the winds come, and let them howl,
With every gust, they'll throw in a growl.
For nature's a jester, with quirks galore,
In the green of their hearts, there's laughter to pour.

Awakening the Quiet

In the dawn's hush, a rustle appears,
A sprout yawns wide, shedding its fears.
With a wink at the sunrise, it stretches out tall,
And calls the dew bugs for a morning ball.

They boogied and wobbled, all limbs akimbo,
While a curious rabbit watched from below.
"Join us!" they cheered, "Come dance in the sun!"
The shy little critter said, "This looks fun!"

Leaves whisper secrets, as shadows sway,
Tiny roots giggle, just trying to play.
With smiles in the breeze and a bounce in their spin,
These green little jesters are ready to win.

Morning's a riot, with laughter and cheer,
Awakening whispers, for all buds to hear.
When flowers burst forth, on this stage so bright,
Who knew seedlings had such a sense of delight?

Wings of New Hope

With sprightly leaps, they reach for the sky,
Bright little wings, they flutter and fly.
'Look at us go!' the young plants exclaim,
'With hopes like balloons, we'll dance without shame!'

The clouds chuckle down, the sun gives a grin,
As roots dig in deep, ready to begin.
Each leaf takes a bow, as they bask in the rays,
For life's just a joke, and they're laughing all days.

With whispers of dreams in green and gold,
The little buds shine, brave and bold.
Their spirits so light, like confetti they twirl,
Spinning through moments, in nature's big whirl.

So spread your wings, tiny shoots, take flight,
For hopes are the candy that sweetens the night.
In the garden of giggles, where sunshine abounds,
Every sprout finds its voice, in raucous sounds.

Radiant Roots

Beneath the soil, there's a party unseen,
With roots having meetings, all plush and serene.
"Best plant puns?" asks the oak with a laugh,
"I'm the root of it all, let's do a quick graph!"

Worms share the gossip, on soil paths they glide,
While mushrooms mingle, all spunky with pride.
"I've got the best view!" shouts a vine with a shout,
"Underground's where the fun's truly about!"

All of them chuckle at the jokes that they tell,
As radishes roll over, saying, "Oh swell!
We'll dance in the darkness till dawn breaks the spell,
These radiant roots have stories to sell!"

So next time you tread, give a nod to the base,
For laughter unearths, and brings joy to a place.
In this garden of whims where nature's the guest,
The roots throw a bash, and it's simply the best!

Roots of Resilience

In a garden where laughter grows,
We plant dreams, and sometimes toes.
With every stumble, we learn to jest,
Roots entwined, we're truly blessed.

A weed may sprout, with glee it beams,
Telling stories of wild, lofty dreams.
Merry mischief in every vine,
Pulling puns from the soil, how divine!

Beneath the surface, chaos brews,
Yet we dance in our mismatched shoes.
In each tough patch, we sow our cheer,
Resilience, dear, is always near.

So laugh with me, let's break the mold,
In this patch of life, we grow bold.
With each new sprout, we find our way,
Watch as we bloom, come what may!

Tender Shoots of Hope

A tiny sprout peeks through the dirt,
With a wink it says, "Life's no hurt!"
Dancing under the sun's warm rays,
Each leaf a banner, shouting, "Hoorays!"

In the breeze, they wiggle and sway,
Looking for fun in every day.
With roots that giggle and soil that sings,
Tender shoots know what joy brings.

When the rain drops fall in playful blobs,
They twist and twirl like little snobs.
Water I need! they cheer and shout,
"Keep bringing the fun, there's no doubt!"

With every bud, the world takes a chance,
To laugh, to love, to sing, to dance.
So here's to sprouts with quirks galore,
Growing hopes that we can't ignore!

Echoes of Tomorrow's Growth

Whispers of green grace the morning light,
With shadowy giggles, they take their flight.
Tomorrow's blooms dance in today's breeze,
Tickling dreams with floral tease.

The garden's a stage, and we're the jest,
Each bud's a punchline, truly the best.
With blossoms that chuckle and petals that jest,
Life's witty script is put to the test.

What's growing now? A vine so spry,
With a snicker, it reaches for the sky.
Leaves that chatter, roots that conspire,
Echoes of growth, our hearts desire.

Among the greens, we gather and play,
Learning to laugh at life's quirky sway.
So pick a petal, let laughter swell,
In this patch of joy, all is well!

The Heart's Quiet Bloom

In a nook where silence finds its groove,
The heart whispers, wanting to move.
A gentle pulse, a tender tease,
In this soft space, we find our ease.

Petals unfold, with a yawn so wide,
A secret dance that won't be denied.
With thumps that chuckle, and beats that hum,
The heart blooms forth, oh, it's so fun!

Among the quiet, cheeky vibes arise,
Holding laughter in every surprise.
With roots that nudge and leaves that tickle,
The heart finds joy in every giggle.

So let it bloom, let the quiet sing,
In the stillness, there's so much spring.
A playful flutter, a gentle swoon,
The heart's bright smile, a joyful tune!

Nurtured by the Rain

Tiny leaves are stretching wide,
Grateful for the drops they ride.
They giggle as the puddles splash,
In their green world, they make a dash.

With every cloud that starts to pout,
The plants throw hands up, sing and shout.
"More water!" cries the lettuce leaf,
As droughts turn garden joys to grief.

Ants march by with tiny hats,
Bringing snacks for all the sprats.
"Pickle-flavored leaf for me,
Hey, who's snagged my cup of tea?"

They sway along in rhythmic glee,
Dancing as breezes set them free.
A rain dance here, a rain dance there,
Nature's chuckle fills the air.

Blossoms of a New Dawn

Morning sun's a silly clown,
Waking buds from sleepy brown.
"Rise and shine!" the daisies cheer,
As they stretch to greet the year.

Bees arrive in polka dots,
Buzzing joy with goofy thoughts.
"Check my moves!" a bee does twirl,
With petals spinning in a whirl.

Dandelions play hide and seek,
With fluff so light, their game's unique.
"Catch me if you can!" they tease,
Before the wind's a playful breeze.

Bright blossoms tease the bumblebee,
"Try this one—it's magnifi-gee!"
With laughter shared and pollen spread,
Nature's party paints the spread.

Gentle Hands of Nature

Tiny trowels in the dirt,
Earthworms giggle, "Oh, it's a shirt!"
Seeds are buried, hats on heads,
While ladybugs play leapfrog beds.

Rains pour down, a friendly flood,
A toothy grin upon the mud.
"Slide with us!" the sprouts yell loud,
"Come join this squishy, slimy crowd!"

The sun sets low, a sleepy ham,
"Please don't cover us!" yells spam.
As shadows grow and giggles pass,
They dream of grass as boats of glass.

Even the stones chip in for fun,
"Let's play rock-paper-scissors, run!"
Nature's laughter fills the green,
Where everything is full of sheen.

From Soil to Spirit

Roots deep down, they tell a joke,
"Why did the carrot cross the cloak?"
To get to the garden where it's bright,
And share a laugh with the aphid sprite.

Sunflower heads do spin in cheer,
"Got a riddle? Bring it near!"
With every turn, they shout so loud,
"Who's the silliest in this crowd?"

Grasses sway like dancers bold,
"Who wants to tango in the gold?"
With each breeze, they take their chance,
Making nature groove and prance.

The soil whispers secrets sweet,
Fostering friendships that can't be beat.
Together they grow, together they jest,
In the garden's heart, they find their nest.

Budding Whispers of Tomorrow

In a garden where giggles sprout,
Tiny sprouts dance about.
Roots tickle the soil with glee,
Whispers of future, come join me!

Dandelions wear crowns of cheer,
Chatting with flowers, drawing near.
They plan a parade, oh what a sight,
Fragrant floaties taking flight!

The sun plays peekaboo with the rain,
Droplets giggle, it's all in vain.
The blooms burst forth in flamboyant hue,
Singing sweet songs, just for you!

With every sprout, a tale to tell,
A tofu tree that grew so well.
Laughter and life in every fold,
In this garden, magic's bold!

Watering Dreams

Drop by drop, the laughter flows,
Plants with jokes, how hilarity grows.
A dash of sunshine, a giggle spritz,
Dancing leaves, in their twirls and flips!

Watering them with dreams so bright,
They tell the clouds, 'Isn't this a height?'
Beans that bend to break out in song,
While carrots claim they've danced along!

"I'm rooting for you!" crows the sage,
Twirling in a comical age.
Even the weeds, with wiggly style,
Chime in the chorus, with a grin and a smile!

Dreams repotted, in pots of fun,
A symphony of sprouts just begun.
Wet socks from puddles, but who really cares?
The plants all giggle, dancing in pairs!

The Colors of Renewal

Bright hues burst in cheerful array,
Pinks and yellows come out to play.
Each petal a giggle, each leaf a joke,
Sprinkled with laughter, the colors provoke!

A bluebell whispers, "Look at me sway!
I'm fashionable today, or so they say!"
While violets blush in playful tease,
Turning heads with the slightest breeze.

Greens unfolding, oh what a scene,
Another party where laughter's keen.
The earth chuckles, as the colors dance,
Spring is a riot; join in the prance!

A canvas of joy, a palette so bright,
Splashing the world in sheer delight.
Nature's artist, with humor profound,
Painting our lives with colors renowned!

A Dance with Existence

In the woods, a whimsical jig,
Trees twirl and laugh, oh so big!
The roots clap hands on the fertile ground,
A comedy show of life all around.

Bees buzzing tunes, with waggles and spins,
Squirrels crack jokes, as nature grins.
Each breeze brings laughter, a ticklish tease,
Dancing with shadows and floating leaves.

The sun struts by, wearing a hat,
While clouds play chess with a cheeky cat.
Life's a hilarious dance, my friend,
From twinkling stars to the earth we tend.

So join the fun in this grand ballet,
Even the stones laugh; they have their say.
In this vibrant dance, take a chance,
Life's just a quirky, cosmic romance!

The Promise of a New Dawn

A worm once dreamed of flying high,
He found a leaf to give a try.
On windy days, he'd gliding swoop,
And landed right in grandma's soup.

The sun peeked out, a cheeky glow,
The world awoke, a silly show.
Birds wore hats, and squirrels grooved,
While daisies danced, all moved and proved.

Yet every dawn, all critters knew,
A daring day would soon ensue.
With laughter sprouting, joy the crown,
Life's little quirks would surely drown.

So onward forth, with glee we go,
In this odd circus, put on a show.
With every dawn, new laughs to sow,
Who knew a leaf could start a row?

Verdant Hopes in Starlit Dreams

In a meadow where shadows gleam,
Worms tell tales, or so it seems.
They sip on dew, light as a feather,
Debating silly things together.

A daisy wished to wear a crown,
While ants rehearsed their tiny frown.
Under stars, their secrets unfurled,
The best-kept laughs in all the world.

A sleepy hedgehog rolled with zest,
Claiming sleep was simply best.
Yet in dreams, he'd race the moon,
And wake up singing like a loon.

So gather 'round, with giggles bright,
In the night's embrace, all feels right.
With leafy whispers, softly gleamed,
In this odd tale, we all have dreamed.

Unraveled Threads of Existence

A spider spun a clumsy web,
It caught a breeze, a woven ebb.
With every gust, a tumble twist,
'Oh, how did lunch become a mist?'

Each thread a laugh, a tangled scheme,
In nature's quilt, each seam a dream.
One leaf declared a bouncy fate,
As acorns rolled, they laughed till late.

A raccoon with a mask of pride,
Passed by a puddle, slipped, and cried.
But even then, a giggle flowed,
While puddle players danced and glowed.

So here we weave our silly tales,
In nature's grasp, where humor prevails.
With threads released, we float and glide,
In this spun world, where joy's our guide.

The Nature of Our Becoming

A sprout once pondered, 'What's my role?'
As snails shared secrets, oh, so whole.
In whispered winds, they found their style,
While frogs debated, 'Who jumps the mile?'

The daffodils with pompous glee,
Preened before bees, 'Look at me!'.
As petals twirled in morning sun,
They bumbled through, 'Life is just fun!'

With roots that tangled, friendships grew,
In muddy puddles, laughter flew.
Rabbits hopped and danced in line,
'We'll be great friends, just give some time!'

In this wild world, we find our way,
With smiles and giggles, come what may.
In leafy laughter, our hearts all blend,
In the nature found in every friend.

Horizons of Heart

In the garden of giggles, we plant with glee,
Worms wearing top hats, sipping iced tea.
The daisies perform in a polka-dot dance,
And sunflowers laugh when given a chance.

Each seed holds a secret, a joke to unfold,
With roots made of ribbon, and stories retold.
We water with chuckles, in moments absurd,
And watch as our plants fly off with a bird.

The breeze makes them giggle, the sun gives a wink,
As petals whisper "Hey, what do you think?"
A garden of laughter, where nature's a clown,
With carrots in wigs, and the radishes frown.

So let's plant some joy, just like we would flowers,
With humor and heart, let's grow happy hours.
In the land of the silly, the sprouts will all sing,
As we harvest the laughter that springtime can bring.

Mornings in the Meadow

The sun tickles flowers, they giggle awake,
Grass blades are stretching, making jokes in their wake.
A rabbit, a jester, in a vest made of fluff,
Picks carrots for breakfast, saying, "That's enough!"

Bumblebees buzzing, a chorus so sweet,
Waltzing on breezes, with tiny little feet.
They joke with the daisies, 'What's the buzz today?'
While butterflies laugh in their colorful play.

A squirrel with a nut hat is hosting a show,
With acorns as tickets, and popcorn to throw.
The pond's filled with frogs that croak out a tune,
In the morning meadow, where silliness blooms.

So join in the laughter, don't hold back your cheer,
The morning is bright, and the fun is right here!
In the heart of the meadow, joy dances on air,
With giggles and grins, it's a sight rare and fair.

Harmony Within the Earth

Underneath the surface, where whispers do play,
The worms are composing a grand cabaret.
They groove to the rhythm, with soil as their stage,
And teach the rocks to dance, despite their old age.

Roots hug each other, like friends in a crowd,
They share funny stories, all silly and loud.
The mushrooms wear glasses, resembling wise mice,
While snails tell tall tales, 'Twas only last night!"

The ants are in sync, they march with great flair,
Waving tiny flags, like they just don't care.
Each inch of the ground holds a giggle or two,
With nature's own symphony, all jovial and true.

So dig a little deeper and join in the fun,
Where laughter erupts, and the puns weigh a ton.
For beneath our feet lies a banquet of cheer,
In the harmony woven, loud enough to hear.

Breezes of Renewal

In the ballet of breezes, the tickles abound,
They salsa through branches, a joy-filled surround.
Leaves laugh with the wind, as whispers they trade,
Drawing smiles from the shadows that dance in the shade.

Dandelions giggle, as puffs float along,
Singing sweet praises, oh, what a fine song!
The clouds join the party, all fluffy and bright,
Shining their joy down, cascading delight.

A butterfly joins, with a twirl and a flip,
Her wings like confetti, announcing her trip.
"Come, join in the fun!" she calls out with glee,
As the breezes embrace, setting spirits so free.

So let's dance with the wind, and laugh with the day,
For renewal is found in the games that we play.
Embrace the vibrance, let the joy flow,
In the breezes of life, there's a humor to sow.

Beneath the Canopy of Gratitude

In a forest where laughter grows,
Trees wear hats as the wind blows.
Squirrels dance on branches high,
Chasing dreams and a cloud's pie.

Beneath leaves, secrets softly hide,
With mushrooms that giggle, side by side.
Each twig whispers a joyful tune,
A symphony played under the moon.

Bunny rabbits trade silly jokes,
While dancing with the playful folks.
The acorns chuckle, 'What a sight!'
In this woodland, all feels right.

Grateful hearts in a leafy glade,
Where every worry begins to fade.
A tree trunk wears its best smile,
And life just feels so, so worthwhile.

Petals of Potential

Tiny flowers dream to bloom,
In gardens where giggles loom.
Bumblebees buzz and play tag,
While snails wear tiny flags!

Petals whisper out their dreams,
While butterflies join in the schemes.
A daisy dons a crown of cheer,
Declaring jokes that all can hear.

Caterpillars munch with grace,
While laughing in this leafy space.
Among the hues of every shade,
Nature's laughter will not fade.

With each bloom, a new surprise,
Smiles awaken in bright sunrise.
Every bud a laugh unspun,
In this garden, we've all won!

Nature's Gentle Embrace

The breeze tickles the trees so high,
While clouds like marshmallows float by.
The sun plays peek-a-boo with shade,
In this cozy nook, fun is made.

Rabbits hop, wearing snazzy ties,
And every flower seems to rise.
A brook giggles, splashing away,
While rocks whisper, 'Join the play!'

Ladybugs wear tiny capes,
As they soar through the air with shapes.
The grass sways like a dancer's twirl,
In this embrace, life starts to whirl.

Every branch knows how to tease,
With every rustle and gentle breeze.
Nature's laughter swirls around,
In this embrace, joy is found!

Threads of Life Interwoven

A spider spins tales of delight,
While crickets croon songs at night.
Each leaf and petal, a story told,
In the tapestry of life, bold.

Worms in the soil wear glasses thick,
Reading the news—oh, what a trick!
Caterpillars knit dreams with care,
As butterflies cheer, 'We're almost there!'

The wind hums tunes no one knows,
While frogs harmonize in their shows.
Roots dig deep, uniting ground,
In this rich web, joy abounds!

Every thread twines a giggle bright,
As nature spins its dance in flight.
In the interwoven, lives entwine,
With laughter and love, so divine!

Caresses of Dawn's Light

The sun peeks out with a grin,
Tickling leaves with a golden pin.
Birds chirp jokes from their high,
As butterflies dance, oh my, oh my!

Morning laughter fills the air,
Waking blooms from their comfy lair.
A dandelion sneezes, it's quite a sight,
Mischief rolls through the early light.

Petals whisper silly tales,
Of garden gnomes and their failed scales.
The breeze giggles through the trees,
Nature's humor puts hearts at ease.

As rays of warmth do gently tease,
Nature's laughter flows like the breeze.
With each soft glow, a joyous plight,
Caresses of dawn's merry light.

Boughs of Belonging

In the forest, branches link,
Like pals who share a drink.
Squirrels launch acorns with flair,
Creating chaos everywhere.

Leaves gossip, whispering low,
Sharing secrets only they know.
A tree's embrace is quite so grand,
Comfort found in nature's band.

Wobbly rabbits hop along,
Joining in the cheerful song.
Each bough beams, feeling so bold,
Wrapped in warmth, never cold.

With every giggle, every shake,
They nurture dreams with every quake.
In laughter and love, they proudly stand,
Together, forever—what a band!

Flourishing in Faith

In the garden of quirky hope,
We plant our dreams and learn to cope.
A worm wears glimmers of gold,
Chasing visions, brave and bold.

Seeds of laughter burst with glee,
Sprouting tales that set us free.
A tomato dreams of being a star,
Wishing for fame, oh so bizarre!

The sun beams cheer when we believe,
Nurturing laughter like a reprieve.
Each bloom unfolds with a funky twist,
In our faith, nothing's amiss.

From root to stem, we sway and dance,
In splendid joy, we take our chance.
Flourishing bright, we find our grace,
With giggling hearts, in this wild space!

The Art of Tending

With a sprinkle here and a dabber there,
We nurture life, a loving affair.
A pruning shears dances with class,
Chopping woes as the moments pass.

Garden gloves donned like armor bright,
We tackle weeds without a fight.
Laughter echoes through the sprout,
As veggies boast what they're all about.

The daisies play peek-a-boo,
As we water dreams, fresh and new.
Fertilizer farts with a cheer,
While ladybugs waltz, never fear.

In this madness, we find our way,
Crafting joy in the light of day.
The art of tending, a wild delight,
Where every moment feels just right.

Tending the Imaginal Garden

In a patch where dreams do sprout,
I planted seeds of wacky clout.
With water from a silly stream,
I watched them dance, a vibrant dream.

The carrots wore a funny hat,
Beets did the cha-cha with a cat.
Tomatoes laughed, their cheeks all red,
While radishes chatted about the bread.

In this garden, joy takes root,
Where every vegetable's a hoot.
With laughter growing side by side,
I tend this space, my heart's delight.

A hose that sings a tune so bright,
Keeps me smiling day and night.
So here I plant my seeds of cheer,
In this imaginarium, love draws near.

Growth in Stillness

In a quiet nook of thought,
I found a place where fun is sought.
Where whispers of the breeze would tease,
And trees could chuckle with such ease.

Mushrooms formed a giddy crew,
Dancing under skies so blue.
While crickets played a jazzy tune,
They swayed beneath the silver moon.

Even roots would wiggle low,
Finding ways to steal the show.
As flowers bloomed with silly names,
A giggle-garden without claims.

In stillness, joy ignites the ground,
With every scratch the laughter's found.
So come and join this playful spree,
Embrace the growth, feel wild and free!

Wandering through the Wild Things

In woods where giggles softly roam,
I stumbled on a merry gnome.
He wore a shoe upon his head,
And claimed it was his cozy bed.

The squirrels held a wild debate,
On who could leap the farthest straight.
With each jump, a feather flew,
As birds cheered on, the gnome just blew.

Through tangled vines and giggles loud,
I found the best of laughter's crowd.
With frolicking fawns and foxes fine,
We painted trees with silly lines.

In this wild place of joy and jest,
Every step felt like a fest.
So if you wander, don't be gray,
Join the wild things, come and play!

The Essence of Becoming

A doodle of a dream took flight,
With silly shapes to greet the night.
In colors bright, it swirled around,
Becoming something quite profound.

With every twist and giggle shared,
The essence danced, it never scared.
The counting stars began to rhyme,
With laughter echoing through time.

While shadows played their little tricks,
The moon joined in with funny flicks.
Transforming moments, gleefully spun,
Revealing joy in everyone.

So here's to growth in every way,
To silly seeds that sprout and sway.
In this essence of becoming bold,
Life's quirks are treasures to behold.

www.ingramcontent.com/pod-product-compliance
Lightning Source LLC
Chambersburg PA
CBHW071835160426
43209CB00003B/314